GRACE KELLY

For Gwyn Yelland,
my daughter,

who tackles life with both
confidence and grace.

GRACE KELLY

THE ILLUSTRATED WORLD OF A FASHION ICON

Megan Hess

Hardie Grant

BOOKS

CONTENTS

INTRODUCTION

Grace Kelly's most enduring gift was making people fall in love with her. Oscar-winning actress, muse to one of the greatest directors of all time, global fashion icon and European princess, she was one of the most beloved stars of the 1950s and is adored around the globe to this day.

DURING HER BRIEF STINT in the film industry, Grace shared the screen with some of cinema's leading men, collaborated with Alfred Hitchcock in classics that redefined cinema, and saw box office success again and again. She was one of the highest paid actresses of her generation and the darling of costume designers and fashion houses everywhere. In just six short years in Hollywood, she became one of the most important cultural icons of her generation.

But just as her star was reaching stratospheric heights, Hollywood's 'girl in the white gloves' gave it all away to marry a real-life prince. She followed her heart across the sea to marry Prince Rainier III of Monaco, becoming Her Serene Highness Princess Grace of Monaco and charming the people of one of Europe's smallest and most well-to-do countries in the process.

Amid the media storm that surrounded her as a royal, Grace was always a picture of serenity, calm and absolutely enviable style. From diplomatic engagements and charity work, to raising three children as a hands-on mother, she showed the people of Monaco what an American princess could do, and they embraced her wholeheartedly.

When Grace died in 1982, a light went out in Monaco and the whole world mourned. Four decades after her death, her presence is still strongly felt within her adopted home, and the worlds of film and fashion continue to honour her legacy. And while her life may not have been quite the fairy tale everyone imagined it to be, the magic, romance and influence of Grace Kelly herself is absolutely undeniable.

THE
WOMAN

AMERICA'S MOST BELOVED PRINCESS was born in 1929 into a comfortable life in suburban Pennsylvania. The third child of wealthy parents, she lived a life of privilege at a time when many were struggling. But an affluent start to life, strong family bonds and a top-notch education didn't inoculate her from the struggles of being shy and introverted, and she never quite fit in with her gregarious, competitive family.

After a childhood largely spent daydreaming by herself while her siblings competed ferociously in athletic pursuits, Grace Kelly set off from the family home determined to conquer the world. She had only one destiny in mind, and took herself to New York to study the craft of acting.

Grace worked hard to achieve success and just a few years after graduating had become a darling of the stage and screen. But her journey to the top wasn't simple destiny. Her success was born from steely determination and a keen sense of her own worth. During her time in New York she built a name for herself through sheer determination and poise, traits that would eventually take her halfway around the world into a role she could never have dreamed of.

Born in Philadelphia on 12 November 1929,
Grace Kelly was the third child of
Margaret and Jack Kelly.

She had an older sister, Margaret,
and brother, John. The family would
later welcome younger sister Elizabeth.

While the Great Depression was hitting families
hard all over America, the Kellys were an anomaly,
living in comfort thanks to Jack Kelly's success
in business and the fact that he had managed to
avoid the stock market crash.

Jack and Margaret were strong characters who had a powerful influence on their children.

Jack was a bricklayer who'd made his fortune in construction. He was also an accomplished rower who had won three Olympic golds. Margaret, a one-time magazine cover model and competitive swimmer, was the first coach of the women's athletics team at the University of Pennsylvania's College for Women. Competitiveness was in the Kellys' blood.

The Kelly family home was a sprawling seventeen-room mansion not far from the Schuylkill River, where Jack could often be found rowing.

The home was made from Kelly Construction bricks and was an undeniable testament to the family's success, something Jack and Margaret were keen to pass on to their children.

Good etiquette was impressed on the Kelly children
from a young age, and they all had impeccable manners.

But despite their outward appearance of decorum –
for example, the girls were required to wear gloves
and hats whenever they were in town – they were
also encouraged to have drive and determination.

Most of the Kelly children would race each other constantly,
leap off things from great heights and play hard and fast.

Grace's siblings were all gregarious and sporty,
but young Grace was serene and introverted,
with a rich inner life.

She shared her siblings' mischievous side,
but a total lack of interest in sport and
persistent childhood respiratory illnesses
put her at odds with the rest of the family.

She preferred staying inside playing make believe to
battling it out in the rough and tumble of the family.

"

ONE NEEDS
to be alone
TO RECHARGE
one's batteries.

"

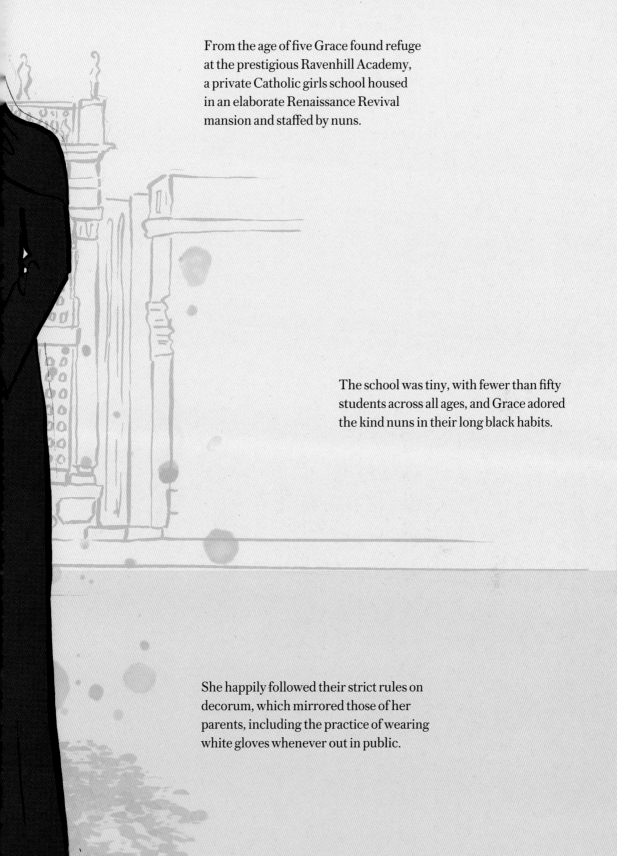

From the age of five Grace found refuge
at the prestigious Ravenhill Academy,
a private Catholic girls school housed
in an elaborate Renaissance Revival
mansion and staffed by nuns.

The school was tiny, with fewer than fifty
students across all ages, and Grace adored
the kind nuns in their long black habits.

She happily followed their strict rules on
decorum, which mirrored those of her
parents, including the practice of wearing
white gloves whenever out in public.

From eighth grade Grace moved to the sportier, more competitive Stevens School.

The school's expectations of excellence suited her – she was a Kelly after all – but it wasn't on the sports field that she demonstrated her ambition. Instead, she dreamt of a life on stage.

Grace was a serious student and showed her dramatic aspirations early.

She became involved in the school's drama society and by the time she graduated had impressed so much that the yearbook predicted she would one day become a 'star of stage and screen'.

Since her immediate family didn't take much interest in her theatrical pursuits, Grace looked to her Uncle George for support.

George Kelly was a Pulitzer Prize-winning playwright whose plays had seen success on Broadway.

He took Grace under his wing and encouraged her early love of acting. He would become a lifelong mentor and confidant, later giving her one of her first paid acting jobs.

George would take the Kelly children driving on Sundays after church, and Grace would insist on always sitting up the front so she could pick her uncle's brains about all things theatre and hear his many tales of the stage.

"

WOMEN SHOULD
have the right to work
AND CHOOSE
the profession they
WOULD LIKE TO DO.

"

Margaret and Jack were keen for their second daughter to attend college once she had graduated, but George encouraged his niece to enrol in acting school.

Grace failed the necessary entrance exams for college, but instead she gained a place at the exclusive American Academy of Dramatic Arts and was ready to take on the world.

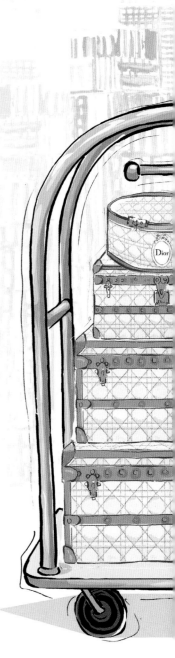

So in 1947 Grace found herself living alone in New York aged just eighteen, blazing her own trail away from her family.

Despite not following her parents' wishes regarding her academic pursuits, she did agree to one of their requests: she would apply to live at the Barbizon Hotel for Women on the corner of East Sixty-third Street and Lexington Avenue.

The Barbizon

The Barbizon had a famous reputation and a glamorous clientele. It was marketed as a safe, respectable home in New York for ambitious young women, many of whom were forging their path in a world that was only just opening up to them.

The hotel's 700 rooms were filled with aspiring actresses, singers, writers and secretaries, all sharing bathrooms and common kitchens as well as a restaurant, coffee shop, library, parlours and a basement swimming pool.

The house rules at the Barbizon were notoriously strict, and three letters of recommendation were required before a young woman's application was accepted. Residents needed to be 'the right kind of girl' – in other words, have impeccable manners and style.

Most importantly for Grace's mother, male visitors were barred from the residential floors.

Grace settled in to the Barbizon and, not one to be told what to do, quickly learned how to get around these rules.

Before long, she was scandalising the other residents by dancing down the hallways in her underwear and regularly sneaking in male visitors.

But in public, as she had been taught, she was always the picture of propriety and class.

GRACE

66

I WAS CONSTANTLY falling in love, AND IT NEVER occurred to me THAT THIS WAS wrong or bad.

99

Grace shared her new home with
a number of models from the
John Robert Powers Agency.

The glamorous Powers Girls were easy
to spot on the streets of New York as
each one carried the same distinctive
black hat box to assignments, filled with
everything they would need for the job.

Before long, Grace signed with the
agency and began getting regular work
in commercials for things like office
paper, toothpaste and face creams.

Commercial modelling wasn't her passion,
but it paid her acting school fees and meant
she no longer relied on her family financially.

She was also a complete natural in front
of the camera, even making the cover
of *Cosmopolitan* magazine in 1948.

While life as a model in New York may have seemed glamorous, Grace's ambitious personality and strict upbringing meant she never let it go to her head.

Away from the cameras she wore a conservative wardrobe of tweed skirts, cardigan sets and horn-rimmed glasses, and she continued to work hard at her chosen trade.

She kept a wire recorder in her room at the Barbizon to practise her diction, doing speech exercises to disguise her East Coast American accent and cultivate the Transatlantic inflection that became such a distinctive feature during her years in Hollywood.

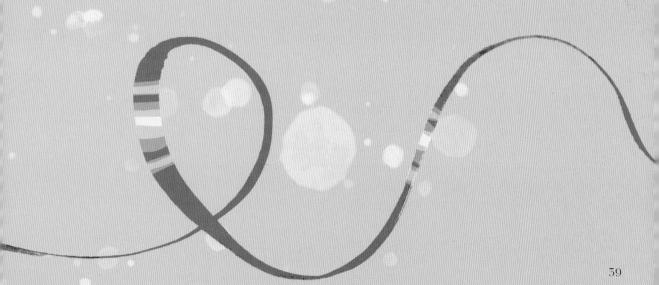

Grace's great love for the theatre meant she had aspirations to work on the stage rather than the screen, and after gaining her degree she was offered her first big Broadway role in 1949, aged just nineteen.

She was cast as Bertha alongside Raymond Massey in August Strindberg's *The Father*.

Unfortunately, voice projection was difficult for the young actress as a result of her early respiratory illnesses, and she struggled to be heard beyond the footlights.

Once curtains closed on the final show, it was back to the voice exercises for Grace. Some say she resorted to putting a peg on her nose and reciting Shakespeare for hours to strengthen her projection.

After her efforts in *The Father*, it wasn't
Broadway producers knocking down
Grace's door, but television ones.

It was 1950, the dawn of a golden era for
television, and Grace's soft voice would be
no barrier in the burgeoning medium.

She worked on live television dramas
and became a regular with the Stock
Company, appearing in nearly sixty
shows over a few short years.

This constant work taught Grace how
to treat acting as a real job. She worked
hard and gained a reputation for being
a reliable cast member.

She also learned how to handle herself in
contract negotiations and was exposed to
the business side of showbiz, something
she would later use to her advantage.

Though she did suffer multiple rejections from Hollywood and her beloved Broadway during this period, Grace's work on television was the first time the world caught a glimpse of the Grace Kelly effect.

A TV producer later recalled that you couldn't work with the fledgling star without falling a little bit in love with her, and it wasn't long before her work on the small screen would lead to a much bigger one.

Grace's childhood competitiveness and drive to succeed had allowed her to break free from her strong-willed family and make it on her own in New York.

Her independent spirit helped her earn a living as an actress, but her determination and drive were about to come up against a force even more formidable than her family.

THE
WORK

NOT LONG INTO HER TELEVISION CAREER, movie offers started to roll in for the striking beauty with a reputation for being a hard worker. The Hollywood studio system was in full swing. Studio bosses and contracts dictated what actresses worked on, where they lived and even who they dated, and Grace was wary.

Grace Kelly would take Hollywood by storm in the six years that followed, but she made sure to do it on her own terms. The shy girl from Pennsylvania starred in blockbuster hit after blockbuster hit, became Alfred Hitchcock's muse and collaborator, and gave the world film moments that would last decades – and she did it all without succumbing to the unreasonable demands of the Hollywood machine.

She also cast aside her sensible tweed skirts and twin sets to become one of the most stylish women of all time, working with iconic costume designers to create looks that became cultural touchstones and honing a personal style still admired today. All the while she would retain an aura of mystery that left audiences wanting more.

Grace's Hollywood debut
was relatively low-key.

In 1950 she landed a small part in
Fourteen Hours, a tense thriller about
a man attempting to take his own life.

Grace was on screen for only two
minutes, as little more than an
onlooker, but she was a glamorous
sight in a fur coat, veil and pearls.

And though she looked lovely onscreen,
it was her offscreen persona that caught the
eye of one of Hollywood's leading men.

Gary Cooper, who visited the set during
filming, later recalled there was something
different about Grace Kelly.

GRACE KELLY

After *Fourteen Hours*, Grace returned
to New York and worked on the stage.
Producer Stanley Kramer saw her in an
Off-Broadway show and invited her to
audition for *High Noon* – alongside
Gary Cooper.

Much to Kramer's amusement, the young
actress turned up to their meeting very
properly dressed, down to the pair of white
gloves she had donned for the occasion.

The habit she had maintained from her
days at school was at odds with the rest
of bohemian Broadway, and it would
become something she was known
for in Hollywood.

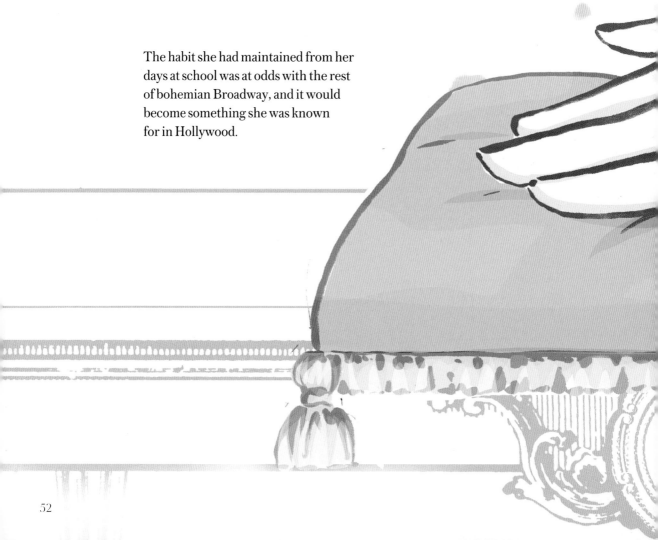

Stanley Kramer never forgot it,
and Grace got the part.

TIME magazine later dubbed
Grace 'the girl in the white
gloves' and the name stuck.

CE

High Noon, which has since been
described as one of the greatest westerns
of all time, was a big-budget epic.

Grace brought a combination of strength
and ladylike poise to her role as Amy
Kane and the film was a huge hit.

With a starring role in such a sensational film, she had seemingly skipped the small roles and low-budget films most junior actors had to take.

At just twenty-two her name was up in lights, but the contract offers that came her way were not up to superstar standard – only $250 a week and far too restrictive.

Unsatisfied with what Hollywood had to offer and personally unimpressed with her own performance in *High Noon*, she returned to New York and vowed to work harder at her craft.

> **"**
>
> # I left Hollywood AS FAST AS I COULD, and I told myself I WOULDN'T

go back until
I COULD CARRY
my own weight
IN A PICTURE.

"

Grace's next chance to impress Hollywood came in 1952 in *Mogambo*, a romantic drama directed by the legendary John Ford. She was required to sign with MGM studios for the role, and they were after a six-year contract at a salary of $750 per week.

Wary of a life dictated by the demanding studio system and still yearning for a career on Broadway, Grace was reluctant.

GRACE

But she was won over by the chance to
star alongside some of the biggest names in
the industry, Clark Gable and Ava Gardner,
and film on location in Africa.

She negotiated a deal with some important
compromises – restrictions on the number of
films she had to commit to, every second year
off to work in the theatre, and the ability to
remain living in New York rather than move
to LA. Importantly, she insisted she should
be able to choose which roles she accepted.

She joked that negotiations had taken so long
she had to sign the contract at the airport with
the plane to Africa idling on the runway.

Mogambo was filmed partly on location near Mount Longonot, Lake Naivasha and Fourteen Falls in rural Kenya.

They weren't easy places to film, and production was plagued by rain, mud and impassable roads. The tense political situation meant the cast and crew needed constant security, but Grace enjoyed the work immensely and made lifelong friends.

She would also earn a Golden Globe and a nomination for an Academy Award for her performance, all but cementing her status as a bone fide star.

With such acclaim, her aspirations of a life spent on the stage were about to be eclipsed by the movies.

Years earlier Grace had done a screen test for a movie called *Taxi*, and, while she failed to land the role, the reel had been handed around to various studios. Alfred Hitchcock got his hands on it and was immediately captivated.

He cast Grace in the role of Margot Wendice, an upper-class Englishwoman engaged in a steamy affair with an American novelist, in *Dial M for Murder*.

For Grace it would be the start of a professional relationship with one of the greatest directors of all time.

Hitchcock was enamoured with his new leading lady and thought her onscreen restraint was the perfect foil for the passion simmering just below the surface. It was a trait he would come back to often in his descriptions of Grace.

DIRECTOR Hitchcock
Grace Kelly

He famously described her as an ice-capped volcano and nicknamed her 'the snow princess'.

65

Hitchcock also respected his new new star's
judgement entirely. The famous strangulation scene
in *Dial M for Murder* was filmed with Grace in only
a nightgown because she insisted her character
wouldn't put on a robe just to answer the phone.

By the time *Dial M for Murder* was released in 1954,
word was spreading about Grace Kelly's X factor.
In April, she was *Life* magazine's cover story with
the bold headline 'Hollywood's Hottest Property'.

The article claimed 'Miss Kelly's cool beauty and
her unquestionably fine acting ability' would
'soon be movie land bywords'.

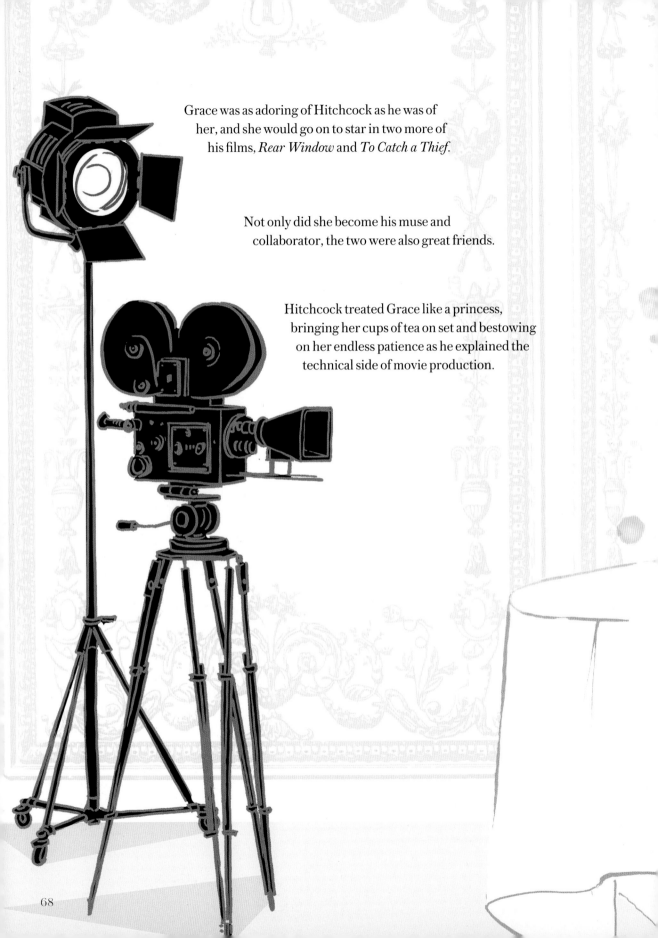

Grace was as adoring of Hitchcock as he was of her, and she would go on to star in two more of his films, *Rear Window* and *To Catch a Thief*.

Not only did she become his muse and collaborator, the two were also great friends.

Hitchcock treated Grace like a princess, bringing her cups of tea on set and bestowing on her endless patience as he explained the technical side of movie production.

Grace often dined with Hitchcock
and his wife at their home.

"

MR. HITCHCOCK
taught me everything
ABOUT CINEMA.

"

It was during *Rear Window* and *To Catch a Thief*
that Grace would meet another famous collaborator.

Edith Head was a costume designer who helped define the look of Hollywood in the 1950s.

She worked particularly closely with her female stars, and in Grace Kelly found the perfect partner.

Grace's striking beauty, model's knowledge of the camera and self-assured approach to fashion made her a costume designer's dream.

'I have never worked with anybody who had a more intelligent grasp of what we were doing,' Edith Head once said.

Hitchcock gave Edith Head more licence than usual when she was working with Grace, and together the pair would create looks that were central to Hitchcock's films.

Grace as *Rear Window*'s Lisa is pure perfection in a New Look–inspired tea dress with black bodice and white tulle skirt.

Rear Window

Grace Kelly

The cap-sleeved black dress she wore in the
same film, paired with a triple string of
pearls, has gone down in film history
as one of the most iconic looks
ever to grace our screens.

"

I favour pearls ON SCREEN AND in my private life.

"

To Catch a Thief was one of the most stylish films of all time. Grace turned heads with every look, while the clifftop roads of the French Riviera provided the perfect backdrop.

The masquerade ball scene was particularly stunning.
Hitchcock had directed Edith Head to dress Grace as a
'fairy princess' for the ball, and Head's gold lamé gown
with sweetheart neckline more than fit the brief.

Hitchcock himself was heavily invested in the visuals
of his films and understood the power of wardrobe –
it was as important to him as cinematography and set.

He was a jewellery devotee, and Grace wore pieces in his films that have since gained cult status. Her pearl charm bracelet in *Rear Window* inspires the fashion conscious even today, and the imitation diamond necklace used as a trap in *To Catch a Thief* was no less coveted because it was a fake.

It was Hitchcock who first introduced Grace to Cartier, taking her browsing at their New York store. Grace fell in love with the brand and started a lifelong relationship with the company.

But though Grace loved working with Hitchcock
and Head, there was still the matter of the MGM
contract she had signed before *Mogambo*.

Hitchcock worked for Paramount, and
Grace was on loan to them for his movies.

Between Hitchcock films she was required to work on
other projects – some she very much wanted to be a part
of and others she only did because she was obliged to.

Ever determined to be in control of her destiny,
she turned down more scripts than she agreed to
and negotiated hard with MGM when it came
to roles she was interested in.

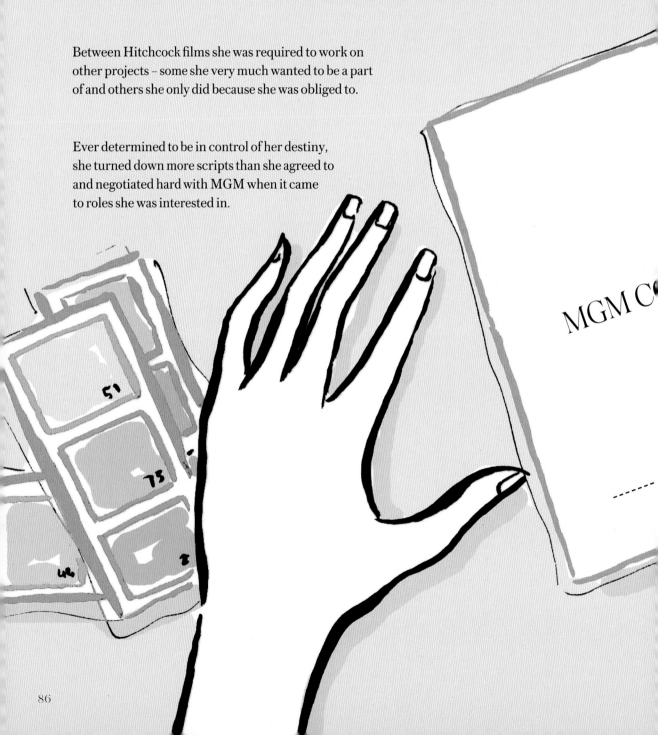

MGM C

But even she had to acquiesce to
the Hollywood machine at times.

"

IF I TAKE ON something, I like TO DO IT WELL and I like to do it COMPLETELY.

"

In 1954 alone Grace starred in five major films.

By the time they had all been released in 1955,
she was the most ubiquitous star in Hollywood.

Her savvy negotiation skills meant she was
also the highest paid actress in history.

The 1954 films included Hitchcock's *Rear
Window* but also the disappointing *Green Fire*,
which Grace had only agreed to if MGM would
allow her to work with George Seaton in
The Country Girl.

Grace had worked with Seaton on *The Bridges at Toko-Ri* and was determined to star in his version of *The Country Girl* – an adaptation of a Broadway play.

The character of Georgie Elgin, the long-suffering wife of an alcoholic, was nothing like Grace's usual glamorous roles and the studio was concerned her star power would suffer.

Green Fire

Grace Kelly

When the production of *Green Fire* was scheduled to clash with *The Country Girl*, Grace threatened to leave Hollywood altogether.

With a steely resolve, she got her way and starred in both.

Grace played the role of Georgie Elgin wearing almost no make-up and a wardrobe that was decidedly dour.

The departure from her usual style was a gamble that paid off: she was granted the Best Actress Oscar for her gritty performance, beating Judy Garland in a shock win.

Grace collected the award in a strapless gown designed by Edith Head – the most expensive dress ever to be worn at the Oscars at that point, and one that went down in history as a red-carpet classic.

'Some people need sequins,
others don't,' Head declared of
the simple column dress design.

Grace would appear on the cover
of *Life* in the same dress later that year.

As her star grew, Grace was taking even
more of an interest in fashion – and fashion
designers were taking an interest in her.

1955
LIFE
NEW RADIANCE FOR AMERICAN CHURCHES
A GARDEN OF SHRUBS TO PLANT NOW
GRACE KELLY.
WINNER OF THE
ACADEMY AWARD
20 CENTS
APRIL 11, 1955

While her on-screen looks were the work of Edith Head and MGM designer Helen Rose, her off-screen style was influenced by American-based couturiers Oleg Cassini and James Galanos.

Grace was even romantically linked to Oleg Cassini at one point, and the pair were briefly engaged to be wed.

But while the relationship didn't last, Cassini's designs would help Grace transform her look away from the screen into one of timeless elegance.

"

I THINK IT'S
important to see
THE PERSON FIRST
and the clothes
AFTERWARDS.

"

Grace was now the Queen of Hollywood,
yet her heart remained in New York.

At the height of her success, rather than buying a house
in Los Angeles like most Hollywood stars, she took over
an entire floor of an apartment block on New York's
Fifth Avenue in order to remain near Broadway.

In 1955, while shooting *To Catch a Thief* on the
French Riviera, Grace had been invited to lead the
US contingent to the Cannes Film Festival near Monaco.

Upon hearing that the American star would be in
Cannes, the editor of French magazine *Paris Match*
proposed a publicity shoot at the Monegasque palace
followed by a tour of the gardens with Prince Rainier III,
the royal head of the tiny principality.

CANNES F

Grace agreed, in a decision that would change the course of her life.

FESTIVAL

The first meeting between Grace and Prince Rainier was nothing more than professional – the prince was nearly an hour late and Grace had already taken the tour without him. But the two hit it off nonetheless, and they began writing letters to one another in secret as soon as Grace was back on home soil.

Their clandestine correspondence continued for seven months, during which time they fell in love.

> "
>
> # I FELL IN LOVE
> with him without
> GIVING A THOUGHT
> to anything else.
>
> "

As she exchanged secret love letters with the prince, Grace was in North Carolina filming *The Swan*, a feature-length fairy tale full of romance and royalty.

Grace starred as Princess Alexandra, a young royal outcast who is raised to be the future queen of a small European kingdom, if only she can marry the right prince.

Dressed for the role by Helen Rose, MGM's Academy Award–winning costume designer, Grace looked every bit the princess she was about to become.

The Swan wrapped in December 1955, and Prince Rainier sailed to America at Christmas to meet the Kelly family and ask for Grace's hand in marriage.

The pair announced their engagement in January 1956 at the Kelly family home in Philadelphia, Grace in a simple polka dot shirt dress, before heading to New York for a lavish engagement party at the Waldorf Astoria Hotel, where she wore a much more elaborate gown custom-made by Christian Dior.

The pair was to be wed in April, but first Grace had one more role to film.

Her last film before setting off for Monaco was Charles Walters' musical comedy *High Society* alongside Bing Crosby and Frank Sinatra.

Grace played a wealthy socialite about to be wed, and Helen Rose designed incredible outfits for her character – none more beautiful than the silk organza wedding dress embroidered with tiny flowers, perfectly accessorised with a floppy wide-brimmed hat and white gloves.

There was one accessory that wasn't from the MGM costume department though – on her finger throughout the film is Grace's own Cartier engagement ring.

At the start of 1956, less than a year after she had met her prince, Grace would leave Hollywood forever to start a new life as the Princess of Monaco, setting sail from New York on the SS *Constitution*.

The grand ocean liner was filled with her family and friends – and two new pet dogs given to her as wedding gifts.

Her old friend Cary Grant had gifted her a poodle
before she departed, and her brother left a
Weimaraner puppy in her cabin as a surprise gift.

Both would bring her great joy.

"

ALL PEOPLE
are capable of
GREAT THINGS.

,,

Eight days after it set off, the *Constitution* steamed into the harbour of Monaco and was greeted by the prince on a yacht.

Escorting him was an entire flotilla of boats, their decks covered with cheering crowds. The harbour was lined with thousands of people welcoming Grace to the tiny principality.

The Constitution

The whole of Monaco had turned out
to greet their new princess.

Sitting high above them on a cliff overlooking the water was the palace that Grace would call home.

The Grimaldi family residence overlooks the Mediterranean from the Rock of Monaco and is known as the Pink Palace because of the pastel glow that emanates from it at dusk and dawn.

As she stepped off the yacht into her new life,
Grace was handed a bunch of flowers by a young
Monegasque citizen in traditional dress.

One report said thousands of carnations rained from the sky.
It was a warm welcome, but, as a foreign national about to
take the throne, Grace wasn't guaranteed an easy ride.

She would have to work hard to genuinely
earn the respect of her new subjects.

"

THE IDEA
of my life as
A FAIRY TALE
is itself a
FAIRY TALE.

"

THE
LEGACY

WHEN GRACE ACCEPTED the prince's proposal, her focus shifted away from the cameras and towards the most challenging role of her life: that of a European princess. With barely any time for introduction, she was expected to learn a new language, navigate the stifling conventions and duties of royal life and, most pressingly in the eyes of the people of Monaco, produce an heir to the throne. On top of the immense pressure to live up to royal expectations, paparazzi followed her wherever she went.

Yet for the next two and a half decades, Grace would handle the chaos that surrounded her with remarkable poise, never buckling under pressure. She maintained her strong aura of self-possession in the face of old European tradition and managed to charm even the most sceptical Monegasques, in the process putting Monaco on the map and using her platform to champion causes that were important to her. Though her heart was forever drawn to the stage, she knew what it meant to be seen as a symbol for Monaco and took on her duty to maintain the image of a princess, never returning to Hollywood.

On 19 April 1956, Grace Kelly married Prince
Rainier III in a lavish two-part ceremony and
officially joined the House of Grimaldi as Her
Serene Highness Princess Grace of Monaco.

There was a small civil ceremony to begin and
then a much larger religious ceremony at the
Cathedral of St Nicholas in Monte Carlo.

It was one of the first events ever televised live,
and 30 million people tuned in to watch across
the world.

Two hundred reporters were in attendance and
MGM made a short documentary of the ceremony
that later aired in American cinemas, ensuring
none of Grace's adoring fans missed the occasion.

133

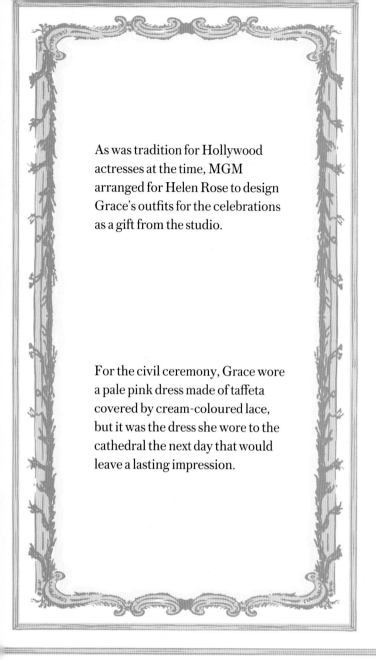

As was tradition for Hollywood actresses at the time, MGM arranged for Helen Rose to design Grace's outfits for the celebrations as a gift from the studio.

For the civil ceremony, Grace wore a pale pink dress made of taffeta covered by cream-coloured lace, but it was the dress she wore to the cathedral the next day that would leave a lasting impression.

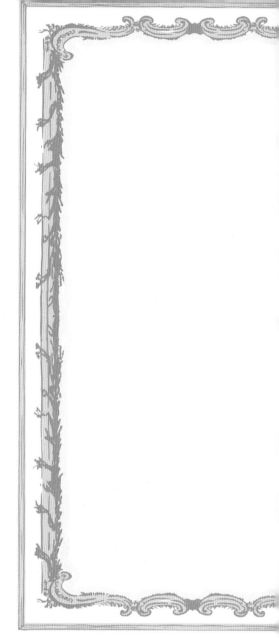

  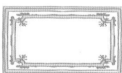 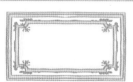

The now iconic wedding gown took more
than thirty seamstresses six weeks to complete.

The finished product was a work of art comprising
25 metres of ivory silk taffeta and 125-year-old Brussels
lace and tulle, embroidered with hundreds of tiny pearls.

With its high neckline, long sleeves, fitted
bodice and full skirt, it was a timeless creation
that has been coveted by brides ever since.

Grace paired the dress with a Juliet cap and
held a simple posy of lily of the valley – inspired
choices that set her apart from the traditional
royal bride wearing a tiara and holding a large,
structured bouquet.

Grace's name was engraved in her
left shoe, Prince Rainier's in her right.

137

"

When I married
PRINCE RAINIER,
I married the man
AND NOT WHAT
he represented or
WHAT HE WAS.

"

After the ceremony the newlyweds drove through
the streets of Monaco in a Rolls-Royce convertible,
a gift from the citizens, before boarding a yacht for a
seven-week honeymoon sailing the Mediterranean.

Once they returned, the real work of being a royal would begin. And, as Grace would soon discover, it wasn't all fairy tale magic.

The most pressing priority for the new couple was an extremely private matter, but one the public took great interest in.

In order to secure the throne for the Grimaldi family, Grace and Rainier were required to have a child.

Without an heir, the principality would return to French rule, and for the people of Monaco that meant French taxes – a very big deal for a population used to living free from income tax.

Grace had even undergone compulsory fertility testing before she could officially accept the prince's proposal and the pressure was immense.

Happily, it wasn't long before Grace was pregnant, but with such overwhelming interest in the matter, she was keen to keep it to herself for as long as possible. In the early days of her pregnancy, she famously stepped out into a throng of paparazzi shielding her stomach with an Hermès sac à dépêches.

While the oversized handbag may have provided some privacy in the moment, the shots were beamed around the world, and one made it onto the cover of *TIME* magazine.

The world now knew about the pregnancy – and the bag, which Hermès renamed the Kelly, has been a coveted item ever since.

This wasn't the only time the princess used an Hermès accessory to unexpectedly glamorous effect. In 1959 she broke her arm while on a yacht and fashioned an Hermès silk scarf into a sling, proving her sense of style didn't falter even in a crisis.

"

Personally, I WOULDN'T GO anywhere important WITHOUT MY OWN favourite Hermès BLACK BAG ...

For me, going
OUT WITHOUT
that purse would
SEEM ALMOST
like going
OUT NAKED.

"

In 1958, Princess Grace gave birth to her first daughter, Caroline.

Her son, Albert, would follow just fifteen months later and a few years after that another girl, Stephanie, would complete the family.

The future of Monaco was secured, and Grace adored being a mother.

She and Rainier insisted on being as hands-on as possible, and Grace became known for the strict but loving approach she took with all three children.

Motherhood and royal duties took Grace's full focus in the years that followed, and she studied the requirements of royal life like she had studied for her acting roles.

With the eyes of the world all of a sudden on the principality, she knew she could use her considerable star power to do good on behalf of the people of Monaco.

Alongside her work perfecting the art of royal diplomacy – learning to speak French and attending functions with foreign dignitaries – she also forged her own path as an ambassador, increasing the profile of Monaco and supporting causes that were important to her.

She established and presided over the annual Bal de la Rose, a royal ball held in the Salle des Etoiles on the Côte d'Azur.

The extravagant event not only raised valuable funds for charitable causes, it cemented Monaco as a truly glamorous destination worthy of the world's attention.

Every year, 25,000 roses would adorn the luxury venue as guests descend on Monaco for a night unlike any other.

In 1958 Grace was named President of the Monaco
Red Cross and opened a hospital in her name.

PRINCESS GRACE HOSPITAL

In 1966 she established Monaco's first day-care centre, freeing women to leave the house for work.

She also remained a passionate patron of the arts: her Princess Grace Foundation supports aspiring actors in both Monaco and the United States to this day.

In 1962 Alfred Hitchcock almost lured his favourite leading lady back to Los Angeles. According to the press, Her Serene Highness would be starring in his next film, *Marnie*.

Ultimately Grace decided to stay in Europe for her royal duties – but for a brief moment the world thought they would see her on the silver screen one more time.

Instead, adoring fans had to make do with photographs of her glamorous life, and the paparazzi were happy to oblige, snapping her in increasingly lovely outfits as she went about her royal business.

Since moving to Europe, Grace's style had evolved again, and she was building an enviable wardrobe, collaborating with designers to create a personal style that befit her royal status and elevated the House of Grimaldi to a new level of refinement.

"

OUR LIFE
dictates a
CERTAIN SORT
of wardrobe.

"

She had developed a close and personal
relationship with Maison Dior since wearing
a Dior dress to her engagement party,
custom designed by the founder himself.

After Monsieur Dior's unexpected death
in 1957 Grace remained loyal to the brand's
succession of creative directors.

When Marc Bohan took the top job at Dior
in 1961, she found in him someone who
shared her vision completely and together
they would form a close creative bond.

DIOR

Dior

Marc thought of Grace as the embodiment
of the Dior brand, with 'a style that caught
your attention but was never excessive'.
Grace would become his muse, and he
a close friend of the Grimaldi family.

DIOR

Grace's love for Cartier never dimmed,
and in time she would also form a relationship
with jewellery house Van Cleef & Arpels.

Both would become official royal suppliers
to the House of Grimaldi and the princess's
jewellery collection would become famous,
as would her enviable collection of sunglasses
and seemingly endless ways of wearing
silk scarves.

Pearls were still a particular favourite
of the princess and would become her
hallmark as she grew into her role.

"

The pearl
IS THE QUEEN
of gems and the
GEM OF QUEENS.

"

But among all the trappings and
preoccupations of royal life, Grace still
longed for the stage and at times she felt
stifled by the traditions she had married into.

Determined to find a way to work again,
she returned to the United States to perform
a series of onstage poetry readings in 1978,
and in 1977 she narrated a documentary on
Russia's famous ballet academy called
The Children of Theatre Street.

In 1982, tragedy struck. Grace suffered a stroke while driving on the picturesque clifftop roads of the French Riviera and lost her life in the car crash that resulted. She was only fifty-two.

When she died, there was an outpouring of grief in Monaco and across the world for the once shy, introverted girl from Philadelphia.

At her funeral, the princess was laid on a quilt of orchids and dressed in a high-necked white lace dress.

In a true sign that she had been embraced by her adopted home, her coffin was draped in the Monegasque flag.

Grace had lived an extraordinary life, filled with kings and queens, heads of state, fashion designers and Hollywood superstars, but it was the warmth and dedication that was evident to everyday people that made Grace Kelly the star that she was.

"

A PERSON HAS
to keep something
TO HERSELF

or your life is
JUST A LAYOUT
in a magazine.

"

With good grace, sacrifice and charm she had won
the hearts of the people of Monaco, and they in
turn mourned her as one of their own.

Her memory now lives on in the streets and hearts of the tiny principality as much as in the contributions she made to the world of film and theatre.

Though her life was public in almost every sense, Grace Kelly had a gift for keeping something of herself private. An aura of mystery surrounded her until the end, and is part of why people are so fascinated by her to this day.

GRACE KELLY

The bricklayer's daughter from America had become an inspiration for all. Her ambition, work ethic and ability to take things in her stride created a model for leadership that has been replicated by royals ever since, and her unrivalled style and undeniable radiance ensured she would remain an icon for the generations that came after her.

"
I NEVER
say never ... and
I NEVER
say always.
"

GRACE KELLY

189

ACKNOWLEDGEMENTS

To Emily Hart for bringing all my publishing dreams to life.

To Martina Granolic for diving head first into Grace's life and sharing my fascination with her incredible story.

To Andrea Davison for so beautifully crafting everything wonderful about Grace's life and seeing this book through to its fruition.

To Staci Barr for your enormous help with bringing the pages together.

To Murray Batten, our tenth book together! Thank you for creating such a beautiful and elegant design to house Grace's story.

To Todd Rechner for your incredible care and attention in seeing my books to their finished form. You've made each book something precious to hold, to read and to keep forever.

To my husband Craig and my children Gwyn and Will, thank you for listening to my ramblings about Grace Kelly for months on end. I can't promise that I've finished discussing her wardrobe in *To Catch a Thief* just yet!

ABOUT THE AUTHOR

Megan Hess was destined to draw. An initial career in graphic design evolved into art direction for some of the world's leading advertising agencies and for Liberty London. In 2008, Megan illustrated Candace Bushnell's number-one-bestselling book *Sex and the City*. This catapulted Megan onto the world stage, and she began illustrating portraits for *The New York Times*, *Vogue Italia*, *Vanity Fair* and *TIME*, who described Megan's work as 'love at first sight'.

Today, Megan is one of the world's most sought-after fashion illustrators, with a client list that includes Givenchy, Tiffany & Co., Valentino, Louis Vuitton and *Harper's Bazaar*. Megan's iconic style has been used in global campaigns for Fendi, Prada, Cartier, Dior and Salvatore Ferragamo. She has illustrated live for fashion shows such as Fendi at Milan Fashion Week, Chopard at the 2019 Cannes Film Festival, Viktor&Rolf and Christian Dior Couture.

Megan has created a signature look for Bergdorf Goodman, New York, and a bespoke bag collection for Harrods of London. She has illustrated a series of portraits for Michelle Obama, as well as portraits for Gwyneth Paltrow, Cate Blanchett and Nicole Kidman. She is also the Global Artist in Residence for the prestigious Oetker Hotel Collection.

Megan illustrates all her work with a custom Montblanc pen that she affectionately calls 'Monty'.

Megan has written and illustrated ten bestselling fashion books, as well as her much-loved series for children, Claris the Chicest Mouse in Paris.

When she's not in her studio working, you'll find her daydreaming about a life spent overlooking the Mediterranean wearing custom Dior fit for a princess.

Visit Megan at meganhess.com

Published in 2023 by Hardie Grant Books, an imprint of Hardie Grant Publishing

Hardie Grant Books (Melbourne)
Wurundjeri Country
Building 1, 658 Church Street
Richmond, Victoria 3121

Hardie Grant Books (London)
5th & 6th Floors
52–54 Southwark Street
London SE1 1UN

hardiegrant.com/books

Hardie Grant acknowledges the Traditional Owners of the country on which we work, the
Wurundjeri people of the Kulin nation and the Gadigal people of the Eora nation, and recognises
their continuing connection to the land, waters and culture. We pay our respects to their Elders
past and present.

A catalogue record for this
book is available from the
National Library of Australia

Grace Kelly
ISBN 978 1 743 79841 6

10 9 8 7 6 5 4 3 2 1

Publishers: Arwen Summers & Emily Hart
Project Editor and Researcher: Andrea Davison
Editor: Allison Hiew
Design Manager: Kristin Thomas
Designer: Murray Batten
Production Manager: Todd Rechner
Production Coordinator: Jessica Harvie

Colour reproduction by Splitting Image Colour Studio
Printed in China by Leo Paper Products LTD.

The paper this book is printed on is from FSC®-certified forests and
other sources. FSC® promotes environmentally responsible, socially
beneficial and economically viable management of the world's forests.